IF...

AARON E. DANCHIK, PRESIDENT
SYNCHRONIZED SOLUTIONS

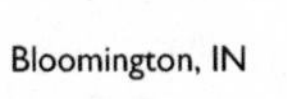

Milton Keynes, UK

AuthorHouse™
1663 Liberty Drive, Suite 200
Bloomington, IN 47403
www.authorhouse.com
Phone: 1-800-839-8640

AuthorHouse™ UK Ltd.
500 Avebury Boulevard
Central Milton Keynes, MK9 2BE
www.authorhouse.co.uk
Phone: 08001974150

First published by AuthorHouse 4/5/2007

ISBN: 978-1-4259-8154-9 (sc)

Printed in the United States of America
Bloomington, Indiana

This book is printed on acid-free paper.

Preface

Everything we do day to day and minute to minute is based on decisions we make. Some of the decisions are good and others turn out to be poor. There is little consistency every time and all of the time. Naturally we believe all of the decisions we make are the right decisions and for the right reasons at the time we make them. The key is to learn from those decisions that turn out to be less than productive and further enhance those decisions that were correct. Once you have found success with something it is necessary to always consider how it can be even better. Think about the outcome. Consider other avenues or steps that could have been added or omitted to achieve the same positive result however, in less time or at less cost. Would this be beneficial in the work place? Would this benefit your personal life? Is your work life and personal life balanced?

In my opinion time management is an oxymoron. There is no way to actually manage time. Time is a constant and we must learn to manage ourselves within time. As such this too affects our decisions, our actions and may influence the omission of action. To a degree time management may be part of the discussion throughout this book. Often times the results of a poor decision increase the amount of time necessary to make the appropriate adjustments and therefore still achieve the results we desire.

Communication is the key to everything. All living creatures communicate. Cultures have unique communications. Animals have unique communications. Humans likely have the most diverse system of communication. Even when we speak the same language consider the outcomes and examples of times where we were in fact not speaking the same language at all. Miscommunication or interpretation is all around us every day. What influences our communications in a group setting? Are there differences in how we communicate in a social setting versus corporate or work setting? Communications is based on our beliefs and opinions. These beliefs and opinions affect our decisions. Some of our beliefs and or opinions have been anchored within us for so long they are hard to dislodge or change. Corrective measures needed to improve our communications skills require change. Fear of change anchors complacency. Complacency is not an option.

Based on the relationship between communication and decision making our lives are shaped. The molding of the proverbial shape of our lives is therefore directly related to our thought processes. Our internal thought processes are manifested outwardly in our expressions as either verbal and or non-verbal communications. The expressions we elect to manifest are based on our decisions we make in processing the information available to us. A person who merely wonders aimlessly in search of excellence and success is hopeful of stumbling across luck. Luck is success to the lazy.

Perspectives and examples provided may be from a managerial role or an employee role within an organization. Goal setting and planning will be discussed with ideas on prioritization an how to approach goals. Communicating expectations will be discussed and how to validate our communications are what we want them to be. Some of these examples may apply to work or personal settings. The choice is yours.

This book is going to take a look at different examples of how the constantly changing thoughts and everyday circumstances we face influence the outcomes of our activities. My intention with this book is to stir thought in the reader. Moving forward please consider and think about taking action steps to enhance your ability to make decisions. What can you do as an individual to realize this potential? Once you enhance your ability to decide you enhance your ability to progress and broaden your opportunities.

There is something on the front cover of this book that is a metaphor for what is within the pages of this book.

Now how many of you actually looked at the cover real quickly prior to coming back to the writing?

Was this a habit based on habit or curiosity? In the event you did not look at the cover yet, you may do so before continuing. The answer to the question is within the text itself.

Contents

Chapter One
The Foundation – Perspective

What Road Do I Take?

Here is how this is going to work. I will define the term in which this book is based and what inspired me to share my thoughts. A brief discussion will take place surrounding my past. This will provide a perspective on my individual opinions expressed and where my thought processes are founded. There will then be a walk through of a day at the office or work. The examples discussed, in this section, are all true. They may not have happened all at the same time and or on the same day but much of it is being translated here as it actually occurred.

Please realize the discussion here is designed to hopefully provide practical examples the reader can relate to within a work setting. Suggestions are merely implied to show how different choices may affect the outcome of our day. The discussion will offer steps or ideas that may be implemented to assist the reader in how they approach their day and prioritize their obligatory responsibilities each day.

My belief is that everything we do in life is influenced and based on decisions we make or those that are made by others around us. When there are decisions made by those around us whom we have a high respect or admiration for we tend to want to mirror their actions. This may or may not be effective in all circumstances for all people. Individually we are responsible for our own decision making capabilities based on our individual desires, wants and needs. With this mind set hopefully established let me share with you a story. This is fictional with an effort to provide an example of what I mean.

A young man worked very hard his entire life to achieve success he had yet to witness within his family. He was the first to go to college and earn a degree. The young man was not without faults and made many mistakes growing up. After college, the young man secured a good job and was responsible. He met a wonderful woman and they married.

Now, as a married couple, the couple had a great life. They shared everything with one another. After being married a few years they were blessed with the arrival of identical twin boys. The couple and the boys traveled and were the stereotypical family. They lived in an upper middle class neighborhood. The family had a small yard and a dog. The mother and father both worked and instilled in their children an honest work ethic. The boys grew up as brothers and best friends.

School started for the boys and they were both excellent students. One excelled in math and science. The other brother excelled in English and music. The brother that was strong in math and science was also the athlete in the family. The other brother was more artistic by nature. Elementary school and middle or junior high school was fun for both boys. They had friends and played sports together. They shared everything as brothers and best friends normally do.

When high school started things started to shift. The brother who was strong in English and music continued to do well in high school and was in many of the honors and advanced placement programs at the school. The other brother was also in honors and advanced placement for math and science as well as on several sports teams. The parents of the boys were very involved with the school and had been very supportive to this point.

The boys entered their senior year of high school with high aspirations to go on to the best colleges and universities for their specific areas of strength. Both boys were accepted to prestigious schools and were looking forward to graduating and making a life for themselves away from home during the summer. They were to both secure jobs to help support themselves while away in college.

One brother moved out of the family home two weeks after graduation to get acclimated to the new community where he was to spend the next four years earning his degree. The second brother also moved out of the house but not until two weeks prior to the start of his schooling. This was the first time the brothers were away from one another for an extended period of time. Both brothers were very close and sensed when the other was feeling down or sick. The brothers did communicate regularly throughout the day, every day on the telephone.

As time progressed one brother stayed focused on his goals and continued with school and earned his degree in four years. This brother set new goals and went on to work in his field of expertise and the field he earned his degree. He eventually married and had three children. His family lived in an upper middle class neighborhood. They had nice cars and appeared to be the stereotypical family.

The second brother had dropped out of school without finishing his first year of college. He did not graduate or keep in touch with his family, including his brother, for many years. In fact, for many years the only time the second brother contacted the first brother was to ask for a wire transfer of money. The second brother did not speak to his parents either. Each time a request for money was made he would be in a different state. On more than one occasion the money requested was to bail him out of jail.

Several years went by and there was absolutely no contact between the brothers. The first brother was in the process of helping his own children prepare to apply to colleges as the oldest was now in their senior year of high school. This brother was still working for the same company he had started with when he graduated college. He was complacent with his life and often referred to his home life as having room mates when he would discuss it with co-workers. He no longer had a relationship with his wife or with his children. The household environment was one of convenience for everyone. This brother was not happy. He missed his brother and the way things used to be. Conversations with his parents were strained as they were getting older and saddened by the lack of contact for so many years by their other child.

The married brother would often describe his life as miserable. He was often depressed and began drinking. He became abusive toward his wife and further strained the family relationship. Financially the family was struggling with three children ready to start college. The parents were non supportive and also depressed. The brother explained to his family he wanted to gather his thoughts and move out for a while. He did so. His wife relayed the message to the parents. This situation only exacerbated the feelings within the home and caused his mother to attempt to commit suicide.

The suicide note found by her body read that she was depressed for many years. She was a failure as a parent. The note continued that she could not keep track of her own children and watched her only child she did have contact with change so much that she simply could not tolerate it any further. She wrote that she never intended to raise a son who would beat on any person let alone a woman. It concluded with a sentence stating she loved everyone in her own way and no longer felt appreciated for her efforts. She did not want to leave a mess so she simply took pills and loved everyone and asked for forgiveness.

Two weeks had gone by since this occurrence and the brother who had left to gather his thoughts called his wife to let her know he was on the opposite coast of the country. His wife explained what had happened to his mother and that she was still in the hospital. She told him that his father found his mother and called 911 to rush her to the hospital. They told the family had she not been found for another fifteen minutes she would have been dead. With this there was silence for a moment and then sobbing apologies and the wiping of tears could be heard through the phone. The man could barely get the words out of his mouth and asked permission to come home. His wife agreed. She promised they could work things out.

The man went to the airport with the few things he had and stood in line for a ticket home. The only option was to be placed on stand by for the next flight that same day. The wait would be several hours. He agreed and went to the terminal area to wait and see if he could get on the plane.

An hour went by and then another. Intermittently he would burst out into uncontrollable sobbing. He was facing the windows looking out onto the runway of the airport. With every plane he would watch take off or land he would think about new beginnings for the people on those aircraft. What seemed like an eternity of silence was soon broken by the loud speaker. The message was a page for him to come to the ticket counter. Hesitatingly with his legs shaking and eyes bloodshot red from crying he approached the counter at the terminal.

Wiping his eyes from the tears he got up to the front of the line. He was informed there was one seat available and asked if he wanted the ticket. He confirmed he did and the attendant asked if this was a last minute decision to travel because the passenger registered in the seat next to him had the same last name. He indicated no that he was traveling alone because his mother was very ill. At that moment the attendant stated, the passenger that will be sitting next to you is a regular passenger with the airlines and a doctor and politely suggested he may be able to offer insight for his mothers' condition. He was then handed the ticket and allowed to board the plane. Disregarding what the attendant had explained he knew he was listening but in reality he did not hear what the words were that were spoken.

He found his row and elected to sit next to the window. He buried his head against the window with a blanket over his shoulder and side of his head. A short period of time passed and he quickly fell asleep. Sleep is often said to be a means of escape and with all he had been contemplating in his own mind he felt at ease with his decision to return home and dosed off. With his head covered by the blanket he awoke when he felt someone tap his shoulder. He assumed it was the stewardess and politely stated he did not want anything and did not want to be disturbed. A voice then said, "I just don't want you to have a stiff neck when you wake up later from being in that position for too long." This voice was familiar. The man sat up rubbing his eyes and was astonished at who he saw. It was his brother. The two men embraced and began to talk.

The one brother indicated he had left home to gather his thoughts and that their mother had attempted suicide and therefore he was returning home. He explained he had a strained marriage and relationship and a job he no longer was inspired to work at. The other brother stated he traveled all over the country and the world trying to identify what he truly wanted to do. He explained he had done drugs. Many times when he had called for money it was because he either wanted more drugs or was in jail for stealing to try and get money to buy drugs or pay off gambling debts.

The first brother then asked how he changed his life around. The second brother then stated that he owed a considerable sum of money to a great deal of people. The money was again for drugs and gambling and he had no other resources available to pay the money back. The first brother then asked how this changed his life. The second brother stated that he woke up in a county hospital in a body cast. He went on to explain that he had been so severely beaten that he was close to death himself. He explained that as he was healing he had an opportunity to think.

The first brother asked, "What did you think about?"

The second brother said, "IF."

With this the first brother asked what about "IF?"

The second brother said, "IF" I had made other choices and decisions I would not have been in the hospital in a body cast. "IF" I had gone to school like the plan indicated I would have a family like you have and you described and shared with me. "IF" I had not made the decisions I made I would not have been hurt so badly.

The first brother then asked about becoming a doctor. The second brother said, because I was so badly hurt, and in the hospital for so long, I had the opportunity to receive care from hundreds of people. Some of them were very kind and courteous and others were awful. I reflected upon my past decisions and realized I had another choice. "IF" I wanted to make a change and help myself and others I needed to go back to school. I did so and became a doctor. Now I travel all over the world helping people recognize opportunities and make better decisions. I had made decisions that affected me, you, mom and dad. The outcome is now I want to share what I learned with others to hopefully make a difference for at least one person. Knowledge means nothing when it is not utilized. Knowledge is only beneficial when it is shared. The knowledge I gained I want to share.

The brothers continued to talk for the balance of the flight and returned home together. The family was once again together and a new chapter was begun.

As I stated at the beginning of the chapter, this is all fictional. There may be parallels with actual families but none that I am aware of. Here there were two brothers that both had identical opportunities to progress. While they followed a similar road to a point in their lives where they each had to make their own decisions the outcomes of those decisions were drastically askew from one another. One brother did what he thought was expected of himself and was not very happy later on. The other brother lost focus and was not happy with what was happening to him and then regained his focus.

The consideration here is for the reader to think about their own personal circumstances. Are you where you want to be? Are you happy? Are you jealous or envious of others'? Do you know where you want to go from here and how you will get there? Do you have a plan? Are you motivated to work toward the achievement of your desires?

Be devoted to your values and desires. Developing true devotion will transform your efforts into rewards. In retrospect it will be the little things that we remember later in life more than the big events. What we think about will come about. Grand dreams are not impossible provided you do not allow them to become unthinkable. Things may appear to be beyond your capabilities. Visualize being in the woods and faced with a grizzly bear. You do not rest while wrestling the grizzly bear when you are tired or you will relinquish advantage to your opponent. Rest when the battle is over and seize the opportunity when the bear rests because it is tired instead.

My focus and intent here is on the way decisions affect our lives. Effects may be personal or organizational. Being we spend more time at work every day than we do awake and at home, the majority of this book surrounds applicability to a work setting. Moving forward, please consider how your decisions affect each aspect of your day. This will be what we look at moving forward.

Chapter Two
My History & Inspiration

In order to start our discussion it is necessary to define the term this book addresses. "IF" is a conjunction with multiple meanings. Because of this fact, the term itself is suspect. We will discuss this and why this is my perception in more detail throughout this book. Meanings include, in case that, granting or supposing that, on condition that, or may mean, even though, whether, when or whenever, and as a noun is a supposition, uncertain possibility or condition, requirement or stipulation. Synonyms include provided or providing.

Let us recognize early that the word "different" contains the word "IF." This is substantial to the point I wish to convey here. Our individual perceptions surrounding communications and our decisions will provide for different outcomes. These outcomes may be based on numerous factors. Without getting into philosophical debates about when a human is truly a human I want to focus on a period when the answer is clear. The period I want to refer to is childhood.

As children choices are made daily. Usually the choices made as a child are based on a desire or want. The choices made as a child can be a learning experience and generally is. The innocence of childhood is a wonderful inquisitive period of time that is often lost as we gain knowledge and grow older. The reality is that the more we learn and know the more we should realize we do not know. We no longer figure the more we know the less we actually know. As children much of what we do is based on negatives. The instructions provided by adults toward children often start off with, "Don't, You can't, No, etc." We continue to make decisions as adults and especially in the work place with negative connotations in the back of our minds. This is where the term "IF" becomes even more important.

I would like to take a look at this phenomenon in this book and hopefully provoke thoughts that will lead, you the reader, to take action. My desire and objective is to inspire you to say to yourself, "Enough is enough. Today is the first day of the rest of my life. I am in control. Today and everyday forward will be different. There are no more excuses. I can take action or omit action, period!" When you do not want to do something, one excuse is no better than the next. Through out the excuses and take action.

I do not know who said, "Today is the first day of the rest of your life." The statement itself is extremely profound and inspiring. We all have challenges we confront regularly at home or work. The objective, in my eyes, is to stay positive. This is more involved than simply stating it. We must live it. We must believe it. We are in control of our actions, our reactions and our choices. Positive begets positive. Think for a moment if you prefer to hang around people who are negative all the time or not. Well, do you?

One of the inspirations I encountered that prompted me to write this book was a discussion I had with a prospect. Before I get into setting the scene, if you will, let me share with you a little bit about me. I believe I have always possessed a positive attitude. This may have been difficult at times as you will find out. In retrospect of my experiences I can think about the statement previously made concerning the more we know the more we realize we do not know things. I am a constant student of my own thoughts and desire to improve. To explain this a bit further I will condense my history to help set the perspective for moving forward with my thoughts. I do not propose my thoughts to be the only thoughts out there on the subject of positive thought. I propose this story to simply be a new perspective, hopefully, in how to approach your own future. It is never too late to make a fresh start and new beginning. Realize here you can not really re-start anything. You end one attempt at something and start a new attempt as a whole new start and beginning.

As a young boy my parents got divorced. My older sister and I lived with our mother and only sometimes saw my father. The situation itself was riddled with high anxieties and frustrations for all three of us in our own ways. My sister struggled with her grades. I too struggled with my grades. For me this was a short lived circumstance. There is more to this that will be discussed shortly. My mother did the best she could and having not been a working mother while my parents were married, at least to the best of my knowledge, she had to get a job. She had limited skills and obtained work as a secretary before transitioning into retail management.

I do not want to focus on my sister or my mother, for now, as I want to share with you my experiences. As stated, my grades suffered and I was highly disappointed with my results the end of the semester in which my father left our home. The situation precipitated the need to move and I had to change schools. The future seemed unsure and the fears unknown. In reality my mother, sister and I moved on average every two years or less for quite some time. The moves were fortunately not too far away from one another so I did not need to change schools again and again or make new friends in new cities. This was a relief. The tension in the home was significant however. In retrospect I realize I was taking action on my subconscious promptings because I wanted something different. I wanted something more. I had a choice to accept my circumstances or create a new opportunity. I had a choice between two options.

Part of these realizations occurred when I was at about eight years old. There was a night or weekend my sister and I spent time at our grand parents' home. For desert that night I had ice cream. When I filled my coffee mug with ice cream no one was close to the kitchen to see me and for every spoonful I placed in the mug I also ate a spoon from the container. You can probably picture this. Sing along, "A spoonful for the cup and a spoon for me. A spoonful for the cup and two spoonfuls for me." And so on. I became very ill that night and did not enjoy the experience. From that time forward I decided not to eat ice cream, cake, candy, drink soda, eat cookies, etc. being in fear of the same result. In retrospect this may have been somewhat of an over reaction however, I believe I am better off for it now. To this day I still do not partake in these types of items.

Back to the school grades that were suffering, it was about the same time period as the ice cream incident. I made a conscious decision to make a change. These two circumstances and the importance they have had on my life since cannot even be explained in brief in this book. I mention this because this, I believe and know, changed my perspective on how I see things today.

My grades improved and I am proud to say I was the first person in my family to earn a Bachelors Degree. I stayed focused on my goals and desires. High school and college introduced me to competitive sports on a whole new level. I had played little league baseball but nothing compared to the seriousness of high school and collegiate sports. This too provided a tremendous learning experience. Running track and field in high school and college was an education in and of itself. If you think education is expensive, try ignorance. More importantly never let schooling be a hurdle to becoming educated. What I mean by this is a degree is important but applying the knowledge gained is where your education means something.

Originally I wanted to play baseball in high school but I did not make the team. Now I thought I was a good player. Going into high school I had played ball for many years in little league and summer leagues to enhance my skills. My neighbor was a professional baseball player on the Los Angeles Dodgers. I thought I was a shoe in. In reality I was not even a shoe lace. My objective going into high school was to earn a letterman's jacket. This was my goal and objective. I decided I would do this when I was still in junior high or middle school. I learned rather quickly I was not a shoe in and, in fact, the shoes were much too big for my feet to fill. Similar to the situation with the ice cream, I did not like the outcome so I tried something different. In the case of the ice cream I gave up deserts. In the case of baseball I tried out for the track team. This was by far the best decision I had made in my life up to that point. The bottom line is I did not like the outcome of a situation, not making the baseball team, and took action to remedy the situation. Once a positive action step was implemented to neutralize the undesirable circumstance it controlled all stress levels or anxieties. This was like a, "Wow, I could have had a V8," moment. I was a fast runner and actually enjoyed running. It was a great fit.

Has a situation ever presented itself to you where you think back now and wonder how things would be different had you taken a different action? This may be, because you are in a better place in your life right now. This may also be because you avoided a negative situation. Think about it and I would bet you there are circumstances you recall that you can say to yourself, "IF only I..." and you finish the sentence. We are all individuals and we are all in control of our actions, our reactions and our choices. This can also apply to a less than desirable situation however I choose not to focus on negatives. With this said let me now share with you what happened to inspire me to write this book.

After spending fourteen years in the insurance industry working in personal lines claims, I quit for a variety of reasons. The reasons are less important for the purposes of our discussion here however, who knows, may be a new book in the future. I had worked my way up from an entry level position handling insurance claims to a management level position. I used to say to people that I made my living off helping other people overcome their misery. Think about it. Someone who has an insurance claim, it is not something you plan for. People do not go around saying, "Today I think I will get in a car wreck and consume many hours of my time in the next few weeks or months dealing with the situation." Aspirations of people are not to be a crash test dummy. We have all probably dealt with an individual in a work setting that you could guess was a crash test dummy in a prior career though. This is especially true prior to a crash. Anyway, I was effective at what I accomplished in that fourteen year period of time and thought I would never leave the industry.

I did leave the industry to start a consulting business. The model of the business is to take consulting to a new level though. I help organizations or individuals identify what they want and where they want to go with their lives or define the results desired. I found this to be only the beginning. Once the definitions or results are identified I do not consult and provide a report to suggest what *should be* done. I help develop the plan and then implement that plan with my clients. This plan is based on my client's buy in and a collective analysis of what is reasonable. This ensures there is accountability and results are generated. There are always at least two options with every decision, to do something, or not to do something.

In hindsight I recognized areas of opportunity. Had I not made changes in my circumstances within the insurance industry I would have been compromising my personal integrity and values. I was not going to sacrifice my mental and emotional stability to benefit someone else. When you do not work on your own goals you must stop to ask yourself, "Who's goals are you working on?" I knew I had to change or improve the circumstances I was dealing with. I took action after evaluating my reactions to those circumstances.

I made the decision I was captain of my own ship. As such, I elect not to focus on anything negative. Sure there will be less than desirable circumstances that present themselves however, once a positive action step is taken to neutralize the negative you have successfully controlled the source of potential stress, anxiety or frustration. This is exactly what I did, when I did not make the baseball team in high school. Although at that time I did not even realize what as happening.

Now in running track I discovered two things. One was I enjoyed the sport. Two was I was actually good at particular events. I believe part of my success was enjoying the sport and my desire to continually challenge myself to improve. My coaches had us go to these classes several times during the week to watch films and learn how to set long term goals and short term goals. I believed the only thing that would help me on the track was to actually run more. Boy was I wrong. In retrospect this was one of the best things I have ever experienced in my life. Every running event I entered, my objective was to merely improve by a fraction of one second. Improvement, however slight is still progress. I could go on but this is enough to give an idea of my background and experiences.

With this stated I was meeting with a prospect and will now set the scene for what prompted this book to be written and my thought process to do so. In this meeting, we met on a Tuesday and greeted one another as would be normal and customary in such a setting. I asked, "How are you today?" The response I received, in a frustrated angry voice was, "Terrible, my whole day is ruined and probably my week!"

Wait a minute. Let us think about this for a moment. A whole day or week being ruined is a waste. There are circumstances we have all dealt with in the past and will likely need to deal with in the future that were or are going to be unwelcome. Personally I refuse to allow something to affect my entire day let alone an entire week. I am not completely immune to such feelings however, I have seen, "The Wizard of Oz." Are you in search of a heart? Do you have courage? I will allow something to affect me for a moment, maybe ten minutes or even an hour. On a rare occasion something may affect me for a couple of hours. Being in control of my decisions, actions and reactions though I cannot fathom allowing a circumstance to dictate to me how my day or week will progress.

Hopefully this makes sense. Due to confidentiality, from this point forward, the information shared is a parallel to the circumstances dealt with after the meeting with this particular prospect. This prospect became a client. The first few days of working together we had several in depth philosophical discussions about reactions, actions and choices.

Since a very early age I have been a partially self taught individual in the relationship of positive thinking and taking action to resolve a situation not cared for. Over the years I have also done extensive research and reading of materials by the leading motivators, teachers, managers, coaches and inspirational leaders in the world. We can look at things as they are and react or consider the bigger picture and then react. This is said because I believe it is important to complete a thorough analysis of a situation before making a decision to act or omit an action. This, as with everything must be maintained in check. Over analysis without making a decision can also be dangerous.

With this said I began to think about the term "IF." The term itself, in my opinion builds in an excuse for any action or omission to act that one considers. "IF" is directly related to our decisions. The context in which we utilize the term may be due to the influences from our subconscious behaviors. Our subconscious has a substantial impact on our daily actions, and reactions.

As an illustration of this I would like you to picture yourself getting on the freeway or highway. You just get on the road and you see a police car. What happens to your right foot?

I bet most of you who are being truly honest with yourself will admit you take your foot off the gas. You may not necessarily touch the brake pedal but you do ease up on the gas.

Why? Remember you just entered the highway and are not likely doing the speed limit yet. Think about this for a moment. Your subconscious overtakes your conscious behavior to dictate your reaction to a visual stimulus. We usually do this because we do not want to get a ticket. We do not want to draw attention to ourselves while driving.

Due to this analogy and the response to my inquiry with my prospect, at the time, I thought about the excuses we build into our daily routines. We will often overanalyze a situation and be hesitant to make a decision or take a stand at all. This leads us to making excuses to delay taking action in hope the situation will go away on its own.

At the beginning of this chapter I wrote about the term "IF" being embedded in the word "DIFFERENT." "IF" implies there is a choice. A choice implies that there is more than one. "DIFFERENT" indicates there must be more than one to create a comparison. A comparison therefore becomes a choice and the choice being reviewed now implies plurality. Thus having more than one available to us is an underlying theme.

Chapter Three
Time Management – Morning Start

Communications

Every morning when we wake up it is a good morning. The morning when we do not wake up at all will present a whole new realm that is unknown and not going to be discussed here. In the morning however, we all have a choice to make. We must all consider and decide between: One, I will have a good day, or Two, I will have a bad day. The contemplation needing consideration is "IF" I choose to have a good day how will I benefit and how will those around me equally benefit? "IF" I choose to have a bad day how will it affect me and those around me? An additional consideration here would be why elect to have a bad day.

When we have a preconceived notion it will be a bad day or difficult day, it likely will. The mind is a very powerful tool. As stated earlier, we are in control of our actions and choices. Because of this, why would one voluntarily select to have a bad day? This just does not make sense. It is often our attitudes and thought processes toward a task that needs to be completed or our jobs that affects us emotionally. When we perceive our results to be menial, at best, we will often perform at a comparably menial level. This perception influences our subconscious behaviors to overtake our rational with emotional responses based on the perception itself. When this is negative, as is usually the case, we adopt a defensive posture toward the tasks at hand. This is due to our subconscious dictating to us to be defensive against the negative circumstance because we emotionalize the situation versus rationalize actions that can be taken to neutralize the threat posed.

Think for a moment of a task you knew had to be completed. This may be work related or personal. Think of a situation that you had a dreaded feeling going into the event yet knew it was something that could not be avoided at all. We have all had these types of events at one point or another. Maybe it was personal and related going to a doctor. You knew you had to go to the doctor but that you also needed to get a shot. Some people do not like to get shots. Because of this you develop a negative connotation and expectation as to how the experience will end. Maybe it was a time where you had to go to court for a ticket. One more example within the work place may be that you were placed in charge for a week while your boss was on vacation. Murphy's Law kicked in with a vengeance. You were kicked with both feet. Both feet were wearing steel toed boots. Monday morning you are anticipating terror when you arrive at the office. Has this ever been a thought process? Why do we set ourselves up for negative circumstances? Why expect a negative?

For a moment let us assume the following was your thought process Monday morning. You go through your normal routine that morning and get to work. Upon your arrival your boss is already there. Hesitant to even approach your boss you do so anyway with a ghostly look on your face. Your boss explains the reports from the prior week were being reviewed and there are numerous concerns. You sink down into the chair as if you are a child being scolded by a parent. Awaiting your punishment and confirmation of how long you will be grounded or unable to watch television or play with your friends, you sit in silence. Your boss then asks you if you learned anything the prior week. All that can come out of your mouth is a timid, "A little." Can you picture this happening? It is like you are six years old all over again.

Your boss then proceeds to explain to you that the results generated were expected. In fact, the results were better than expected. You breathe a sigh of relief. Your boss continues by stating that this was a learning opportunity for you to develop your skills and is grooming for advancement with the organization. All of a sudden you have a new perspective as if your eyes were interchangeable and you are seeing things through a new set of eyes. You become a magpie and regurgitate volumes of information, most of which has no relevance, regarding the prior week. Your perspective changed when you realized you would not be grounded. The question therefore becomes, why did you think negatively to begin with and assume the worst?

Now consider the term, "IF" and think about your approach to the day. Ask yourself how you could have prepared for the day differently. Different encompasses "IF." You could have approached the situation something like this. What I am about to share with you I share with many of my clients and the personnel I work with that actually report to a manager or supervisor. When you recognize something has not been completed or gone wrong, do not wait for the information to be discovered by someone else. Bring up the issue on your own. Take ownership of the situation. Eat the steak before it sizzles.

Here is my suggestion, as an employee. Go into your supervisors or managers office and say, "Boss, I have identified an area of opportunity for myself to be more productive at my job. A situation came up and I did the best I could but believe I made an error." Explain what you did and most importantly offer a solution. At a minimum express how you would do things differently in the future should the same situation present itself and ask for input or commentary on whether your suggestion is valid and would be a better approach moving forward. I guarantee you will earn a new level of respect from your superiors.

In the prior example what would happen by stating, "Boss I appreciated the trust and confidence you placed in my abilities last week while you were on vacation. Thank You. I believe I learned quite a bit that will help me perform better at my current position. I believe I may have fallen short of some of the expectations you had for me however I have a new appreciation for you and your responsibilities here. I feel I will be more efficient and successful in my position here. Thank you again for the opportunity."

Now let us look at something from a new angle. As a leader, a supervisor, manager or executive you have the responsibility to recognize your staff equally. What I mean by this is to be visible and set an example for entry level staff to management level and top performers equally. Visualize, in a work setting, management greeting senior staff and top performers in the office and possibly brand new employees, only. The management says hello and asks how they are doing or how they spent the past weekend. Management that shows genuine interest in their staff will likely have a more loyal and happy staff. The employees that do their jobs but do not exceed established expectations and therefore are not readily communicated with will create an imbalance within the office. Recognition is necessary and mandatory to create an environment that is inviting and cultivates camaraderie. Everyone wants to feel appreciated. People deserve courtesy. When this is not present the division of feelings and perceptions as to the effectiveness of management can be split in two realms. One being those staff members that are recognized and the other realm being those staff members with the perception they are being ignored or not valued by the organization.

In the event you are not in management or a supervisor and are in fact one of the employees within a business, think about your personal morale level. Is your morale level consistent? When your morale level changes have you stopped to consider the cause of the change? Think about your current position or a prior job and the analogy presented. Why did you leave your prior job? Was it for more money or a better opportunity? Did you receive the level of support and encouragement you needed? Were you made to feel as though you were valued or a commodity and that management had no intention of helping develop you in your professional role? Maybe you graduated and it was simply time. The point is, you can likely think of a time where you made a change in your personal circumstances due to your perception relating to the situation itself changing. This may be similar to a change in a relationship and not necessarily a job. Perceptions change. Is your job something you are excited to go to in the morning?

Now let us approach an idea from a practical perspective and consider from here forward how we approach our day. We will begin with the start of the day and continue our discussion moving forward with various parts of a normal day at work. The examples are designed to be somewhat generic as this book is not intended to be industry specific. These bits of information are mentioned, periodically, to establish or share my perspective and express my opinions. After fourteen years in a corporate setting before starting my consulting and business coaching endeavors I have witnessed every circumstance that is represented here. Many of them have been experienced more than once.

We will start with the beginning of the day. Everyone goes through a unique process in the morning. Let us take a look at some suggestions that may be implemented to start the day in a better mental frame of mind. Think about your individual routine each morning. It may be different on the weekends or non work days. For purposes of establishing a protocol let us assume for a moment that the routine is to get up in the morning and walk the dog. You get up and put on some sweats and go for a walk. Upon returning you start the coffee and then take a shower. After a shower you get dressed and brush you teeth. You get the idea. You generally will follow the same steps every morning with little or no variation. This is normal. Think about what you do daily and the order in which you do it. Does your routine vary? When you walk the dog or drive to work or school each day, do you take the same route? Do you mix it up just for fun? I propose you are more a creature of habit than you realize. Until it is brought to your attention you likely do not think about your routine. Consider your coffee and how you drink it. Do you always use sugar or milk or does it too vary?

Now let us compare two days. This implies there may be a difference due to a comparison. Remember, "DIFFERENCE" houses "IF" and influences decisions. Change thoughts for a moment and think about a work day that was less than desirable. Also think about a work day that was absolutely fantastic. Did your actions taken to start these days differ substantially? Probably not. We are creatures of habit. So consider why some days are better than others. Think about who greeted you upon arriving at your office. Did the boss come around and say good morning? Are you the boss and did you greet everyone with equal enthusiasm when they walked through the door? Were bagels or donuts delivered by a vendor thanking your office for a job well done? Usually recognition tends to put us in a better mood. We like to and thrive on being thanked. The perceived value behind being recognized by those in an authoritative position within the work environment is motivating. This will be discussed more later.

A critical element in training ones self to have a great day is to put into practice the thought process that you are in control of you own decisions. As such, select to have a great day. It really is as simple as that. Why self impose limitations upon yourself that can negatively influence your actions later on? Every circumstance that we deal with allows us to view things in multiple perspectives. Communications is often hindered because of the inability to recognize perceptions and anticipate reactions from the recipient of the communication. There are opportunities all around us. It is how we select our reaction to those opportunities that will further our cause or hinder it. Communication skills can be developed.

I meet many people who are extremely analytical and almost to a fault. There are times where it is important and proper to do your due diligence and not react hastily to circumstances. Taking into consideration all possible variables that will affect the outcome of a scenario is crucial to sustained success. To not make a decision at all can be very costly too. We must be cognizant of the effects of our decisions. Make decisions quickly upon having the information necessary to do so. There may be times where the decision made is not the best however, this will allow for you to take new actions and know what does not work. This changes the focus from being on a negative to a positive. With this in mind you can now repeat the tasks more intelligently and ensure the desired outcome. Another option when a decision is found to be incorrect is to merely give up with a defeatist attitude. I can promise you one thing this will definitely not help further your cause.

This discussion started with how you approach your morning. Now I would like to propose to you that you take control. After all, you are in control of your decisions, actions and reactions to situations. In working with a new client I recently went to lunch with two of the managers. I worked with their office for several weeks to gather information. I often describe this as being in "Colombo" mode when I am fact finding. I felt it was necessary to define a plan to help them based on the information gathered and proposed to first eliminate the negativity apparent in the office. With this, one of them asked me, "How do you always stay so positive? And how can we do that?"

With the question posed the response was quite simple. I explained to them, I choose not to be negative. I choose to wake up every morning and be grateful that I actually woke up. I look around my home and I am grateful for what I have. I do not show jealousy for what other people have. Keeping up with the Jones' was never my style to begin with. Just because someone else has a more expensive car or larger home does not mean that they are in fact happy. I then shared something my grandmother would say all the time. She had a saying, "It is better to be dancing on the daisy's then pushing them up." This is how she started every day. This is a wonderful mindset. It is simplistic yet very powerful when you think about it.

There are so many things that occur that become a drain on one's mental state. This is not necessary. Once we make a decision that we do not want to deal with a negative circumstance and we proactively take actions to resolve the issue we have neutralized any threat it may pose. Now I am not insensitive to the fact there may be more significant issues that one must deal with from time to time. My point is a positive perspective will allow you to open more doors of opportunity than a negative perspective. The belief you will be worse off than your current state if you take any action at all is not productive. When you are not finding the circumstances or opportunities you want, create them.

Part of being able to develop this skill is to want to do it. The other part of the skill is to develop a habit of writing down your plan of action on a daily basis. We all have numerous tasks we complete during the day. I would venture a guess the majority of those tasks are not written down. By not doing so you are depriving yourself of earning credit for the completion of those tasks. We all enjoy the feeling of accomplishment but deprive ourselves of seeing our efforts when we do not keep track of everything that we do.

I can almost guarantee at some point you or someone you know has stated, "I have not been able to get anything done today." When we stop to look at this statement and what it represents we would have to be asleep the entire day to remotely come close to this being reality. In the event we were asleep for twenty-four hours and we really want to break things down, we would be doing something, sleeping. My point here is that we must write down and track what we do and be proud of even the little things that seem insignificant.

Planning develops the skills to follow directions, not leave anything out, and keep track of your time needed to accomplish your goals. What I am suggesting may be done at the end of the day or each morning when you wake up. This is something that is individual to each of us. The idea behind what is going to be shared is to do this regularly and in sequence each morning just as your routine is now for getting up and ready for work. Do you shower and then brush your teeth or brush and then shower. By thinking about this subconscious behavior you will likely realize you go about these tasks the same way all of the time or at least most of it. I want you to add one small step.

Build into your routine "Me Time" to reflect upon what it is that needs to be accomplished that day. You will make a list of your tasks and in this process I suggest you prioritize at the same time. This will become easier with practice and repeated implementation of the process. Identify what tasks will have a negative consequence should they not be completed. These items go on the top of the list. Include on your list all tasks however minute you may feel they are. Include on your list, for example, getting gas in the car or going to the bank and dropping off the mail at the post office. Include items such as walking the dog or watering the house plants. At first your list will continue to grow. As you complete tasks that were not on your list to begin with, write them down as well. I highlight my tasks as I complete them. Other people will put a check mark next to them. I do not advocate crossing the item out as you may not be able to read it later or refer to it again if necessary. Calls that need to be made should be listed with the person's name and phone number so you do not have to search for it later. Develop a legend, of sorts, to indicate a positive phone call, a message was left or possibly something to indicate they were not interested. For this I use a minus sign and move on. Design something that makes sense to you. Keep it simple.

With this completed you will track what your activities are. Set up a check point for later in the day to ensure you are on track for your daily goals. This is also true for your weekly, monthly or quarterly and yearly goals. We will discuss more about this shortly when we discuss a mid day check. At this point I want you to think about the term "IF" again.

"IF" can influence your day positively or negatively depending on your individual perspective. As stated, consider the consequences of not completing a task. "IF" this is not done, what will happen? As human beings we contemplate and play with the term "IF" in almost everything we do. Why? In some cases we may be setting ourselves up for an excuse or way out if you will. "IF" is one of those terms that allow you to play both sides of the fence. You are playing both offense and defense at the same time. You are indecisive. You may as well go around saying I used to be indecisive, but now I am not sure. Make decisions and learn by those that prove themselves to be incorrect and move on. You will not repeat what does not work and eliminate these circumstances from future attempts. Do not dwell on a situation. Remember that straddling the fence will require great balance. This may not be an issue most of the time or until you are fatigued. When you feel fatigue be very careful or you will risk serious injury should you slip.

By prioritizing your tasks and your day you keep on target. Focus on the big tasks first. To complete the quick or easy tasks can create fatigue to detract from the intensity needed to conquer the larger projects. This may also result in pushing a project or task forward and sooner or later it becomes a factor in your thought process each morning on whether you will elect to have a good day or a bad day. Anticipatory anxiety of the tasks ahead can be detrimental to success. Think about the earlier example of going into the office on Monday morning after your boss being away for a week.

Once you complete the larger projects, first, and then start to power through the small stuff you will gain momentum. Visualize a bicycle. A bicycle needs two things to move forward; one it requires balance and two momentum. Without balance the bicycle will fall over. Without momentum it will not progress and makes balancing more difficult. Without this the bicycle will also fall over.

With the activity of highlighting what is completed I can still read my notes. What I have done is easily able to be referenced. Later in the day should I feel a bit fatigued I can reference my list to see all of the things I have accomplished versus what is still needed to be done. This is a motivation for me. When I see I have done two thirds of my list of tasks by lunch time I am in a good mood. I am making progress. This has a positive affect on my outward expressions to my boss, co-workers, customers, etc. People can perceive when someone is having a bad day. When you are getting things done there is no reason to have a bad day. Stagnation does not have to be permanent. Slow progress is better than no progress at all. When you have created your own momentum your bicycle is balanced and easier to ride.

I can understand having a bad moment or maybe even two. This may extend to a bad hour or even two. I choose not to allow an unfortunate circumstance dictate that I will have a complete day that is awful. I am in control. You are in control. Negative thoughts can only enter your mind if you let them. When you open the door to your mind you are letting the future in. The future is what you make of it. Do you see the problems in every circumstance or the opportunity to learn and do your best? We are often so caught up in our routine that we do not realize what our surroundings actually are. We are less appreciative of what we have. A fish does not know it lives in water until it is in the boat. In order to become a big fish we must learn to recognize when to open our mouth and when to keep it shut so as not to be hooked.

When I was a manager of a team I would always say there are no problems, only solutions. Anything presented to me was viewed as a puzzle. My perception is that I like puzzles. I do not fear puzzles. The objective is to solve the puzzle. Day to day activities is a game. Your objective is to play the game to the best of your abilities and win. Winning may be completing the steps to the game faster and more efficiently. This all starts with your attitude you select when you wake up in the morning. Your perspective you elect to adopt each morning is a decision. Just as getting dressed and deciding if you will wear blue, black or brown, you adopt your attitude and perspective. "IF" is therefore a decision you make on a daily basis. "IF" is a decision you make throughout the day.

Chapter Four
Mid Day Check Point

Are You On Target?

Now I want to focus on a time frame where things are settling down and you are likely in a groove at work. Every day, late morning, develop a protocol to perform a status check. Similar to your habits of how you get ready to go out of the house everyday, you should insert a five to ten minute status check point in your schedule. When you are planning your day this should be scheduled as a specific appointment. We are all usually pretty good about keeping our appointments. To not do this we could impact our image we project of ourselves to others. This is another "Me Time" you set aside to ensure accountability to yourself.

This check point time will allow you to see how many items on your list are checked off or highlighted. Are you on track? Are you ahead of schedule? When it is discovered you are ahead of schedule it is not the time to sit back and get lazy. Just the opposite is true. You are being effective and efficient. Ride the momentum and balance on the bicycle to do even more. Go further and stretch yourself. You will never know how far you can go if you do not test yourself and look back to see how far you have come. In any corporate type environment your job or position likely has job duties associated with the title you hold. To complete those duties is to do your job effectively. Is anyone truly deserving of a pay raise for simply doing what there job is? I will likely get some type of feedback from this question. The point is that when you are being paid to do a job and that is all that you do, you are being compensated as described in your employment agreement with your boss.

Take this to the next level. You have just completed your check point of the tasks you know you must complete for the day and realize you are ahead of schedule. You complete two more items that would have otherwise waited until after lunch. You are cooking with fire. You are on a role. You have the balance and momentum on the bicycle and go to lunch. You return from lunch and power through the last few tasks you had on your list. You express a big sigh of relief that you are on track for completing everything you needed to during the day and you feel great. For the last hour and one half at the office you rearrange the pens and pencils in your pencil holder on the desk fifteen times. You tried to place them strategically around the rim of the holder. You tried to alphabetize them by color or the name of the vendor on each pen. You also tried to organize them by height and finally by the amount of eraser that is left on the pencils. You have gone from being productive to nothing more than a seat warmer. What happened? Why have you lost focus? Are you completing the tasks your job requires or going above and beyond? Where is the proactive initiative to raise the bar? You were cooking with fire and now you can not even smolder. You have gone cold.

With this activity, or lack thereof, your boss walks by. Your boss inquires as to what you are doing and you indicate, "I am cleaning my desk to be more efficient." Your boss looks at you with the yeah right expression on his or her face and says how long have you spent doing this? You reply about one half hour. Not realizing there is still almost one hour to work your boss asks if you completed all your work for the day. You respond affirmatively and then the boss says, "Great, come with me." Grand thoughts run through your mind that the boss will reward you for completing everything you needed to complete for the day. You figure he or she will compliment you for taking the initiative to clean your work station or area. You feel the imaginary pedals of the bicycle moving with minimal effort. You are visualizing yourself coming to the top of a hill. The hill drops over a mile downward to a lovely park. There are trees, a lake, kids playing, fun being had by all. You further visualize stopping at the park after coasting down the hill the entire way. Once there you sit back on a park bench and watch the birds in the lake to wait for the day to end in a state of relaxed euphoria.

Realizing your day dream must temporarily come to a halt you follow your boss into his office and the door closes. Your thought process is you will now get your reward. All of a sudden BAM! Your boss slams a fist on the top of the desk and asks in a frustrated voice, "What the heck are you doing? Do you think I am a monkey in this suit? You are pulling my leg, you need to switch and pull on the other one because the one you have is getting too tired." Your sense of lost euphoria turns to sarcastic humor. You figure your boss does not like their bicycle anymore because it is "two tired," and they do not understand.

Your perception of euphoria has just changed. You think quickly to yourself, "IF" my perception was different maybe my reaction would be too. That dreaded “IF” word creeps up again. Your boss then says come with me and motions to follow him or her. Thoughts of now what are running through your mind and it has started to rain on you sitting on the bench enjoying the park. You now think about riding the bicycle up hill for a mile in the rain. The euphoria has ended.

You follow the boss into the supply room and because or your efficiency in completing your work on time and wanting to clean up your work station you are assigned to clean up and organize the supply room. The supply room looks like the bedroom of a ten year old where the closet Gods threw up. You can envision being at your desk working on other projects but now have this task to do and no motivation to do so. A short time earlier you were so pleased with yourself for getting your work done. You then had day dreams and thoughts of relaxing at the park. You then think about tasks you need to work on for the next day and realize you could have started them to get a jump start on their progress. Your little voice in your head starts to do laps yelling as loud as possible, “IF, IF, IF, IF.” You became complacent and this lead to a lack of focus on other aspects of your job you could have been doing to exceed expectations for the boss and company.

“IF” you had approached your boss to say, “I am ahead of schedule are there other employees that are not caught up that I can help, would that be acceptable to you?” the outcome may have been different. Maybe you would simply start the other projects so when your boss came by your desk you could have stated you were ahead of schedule and started the projects for the next day. You could have also pondered the thought to ask your fellow employees if they needed help. Chances are when your boss came around and asked you what you were doing and you were at a co-workers desk you could have replied I am helping out here because I was ahead of schedule and completed everything I had on my "to do" list today. This expressed action, of which you have control, now shows you going above and beyond the pre-defined job duties and taking the initiative yourself. This is a positive action and a proactive approach. Likely this action would prevent you from having to clean up the proverbial puppy presents left on the lawn of the supply room where the closet Gods just threw up as well.

There are always two points of view and two ways of looking at a situation. The example above is trying to illustrate that "IF" another choice was made the outcome and potential benefits would be completely different. Taking into consideration the cause and effect of our actions or omissions to act in a given circumstance may have profoundly opposite consequences.

To develop a protocol for your self, to have time prior to the lunch break at work, to evaluate the progress one has made is crucial to sustained success. Let us assume for a moment, "IF" the circumstances described were completely different, to the degree that you were far behind and not on schedule to complete everything on your list. In the eventuality this was presented, the decision to go to lunch where you know the time required would be a full hour, or simply going for a lunch that was a bit faster to allow you to return to your task list would have affected your decision of where to go for lunch. "IF" is a powerful word and thought that is seldom taken as seriously as it should be. "IF" implies there is an excuse or an out built into a situation. Contingency plans are prudent to have but not at the expense of sacrificing efforts to begin with.

Outcomes in a variety of circumstances are dependent on the choices we make. Time is a constant. We do not manage time but we manage ourselves within time. The day has twenty-four hours. It does not matter whether we are a student, doctor, lawyer, business person, employee, employer or whatever. Time is the same for all of us. Few of us, invest time. Perceptions tend to be that time is a commodity. I would love to meet a person who can actually make time. Should such a person exist, besides someone who literally builds clocks or watches, I would like the recipe. For those who have disposable income and think they can buy time, I would like the contact information of the supplier so I may buy a dozen.

"IF" is an interpretation by itself. "IF" someone could truly make time what would that mean? Where does time live? Where is time? Aside from a constant what is it? Is time tangible? These questions and more can be taken into consideration and debated. The debate would surround the term "IF." There would likely be two sides to the debate. One side will argue that time can be found, purchased, made, etc. The other side will argue time cannot be found, purchased, made, etc. "IF" one or the other. Who is correct? "IF" a chicken can lay an egg, and the egg is necessary to hatch the chicken, which came first. "IF" is a term that can cause tremendous debate.

So it is at this juncture that we review the facts. In the morning when we all get up we have a choice. We choose "IF" we will have a good day or a bad day. Just prior to lunch time, "IF" we are on track for meeting our daily objectives or not needs to be verified. "IF" we select particular mind sets or attitudes over others and "IF" we stay focused on the tasks on our lists or not will affect the outcomes of what we want. What we want to do is not always what we need to do. What we think will be the result of our efforts and what will be the results of our efforts are drastically different depending on "IF."

With a plan that is put in writing, as discussed, we have a foundation to build upon. Alterations may take place as decisions are made that do not meet our standards. This affords the opportunity to do something over more intelligently a second time. "IF" we did not have this opportunity we may complete the project sooner however, the project would not be what we initially intended it to be. What we think it will be and what it ends up being, having the opportunity to adjust for variables, are two different things.

Whatever we think we cannot do is probably correct. Whatever we think we can do is usually seldom attempted because of "IF." "IF" the desired result is achieved from my action it will change everything. We may then think, I do not like change. Human nature causes us to place limitations upon ourselves. Consider then, "IF" there were no limitations and you could do anything you wanted to do, what could you accomplish. What would you achieve? Where would you go? What would you buy? What car would you drive? Where would you live? This can go on and on. We often create our own roadblocks. Self imposed hurdles and obstacles we establish for ourselves are an "IF." In other words they are an excuse. We do this in an effort to build an escape route for ourselves. "IF" it does not work this is why. Then low and behold the goal we wanted to achieve, that is not achieved, can be rationalized that it was not reached because..."IF" we had only done things differently it would have worked.

Having an escape route to avoid disaster is important to avoid a storm, fire, earthquake, flood, etc. Building an escape route for our goals is building a foundation for a building on sand. Should there never be a wind or storm the building will survive. In the event there is any natural event and the building falls because the foundation was not stable, it will be stated, "IF" the building was secured deeper into the ground or built elsewhere altogether it would not have fallen. Natural disasters are a force of nature we must be prepared for. This may be one area in which "IF" applies. "IF" there is a natural disaster we know we are supposed to have a supply of caned food and water available with clothes, flash lights, batteries and other essential items to survive. This is likely the only time "IF" is appropriate.

Consider this for a moment. Having all of the paraphernalia set aside for a natural disaster simply shows preparedness and confirmation a decision has already been made. This, therefore, eliminates "IF." Under this perspective it is known what is available and what is necessary to be done in a specific circumstance eliminating the contemplation of "IF."

"IF" is Intentional Fabrication. This is actually a subconscious behavior brought to a conscious level without realizing it. We intentionally fabricate our ideas and excuses "IF" and when we need to utilize them. This is all based on perspective. Our subconscious activity convinces our mind to have an arsenal of responses available if we are questioned. Think back to a time when you knew you would be confronted by a parent, teacher or boss. A situation where something that was expected to be done was not done or an expectation was not met and you were going to be questioned. Assuming you knew the event was going to take place, how many times did you contemplate what you were going to say? How many scripts or drafts did you prepare in response to the situation?

This activity was based on "IF." You began to second guess your first response to create additional responses to why the set expectation was not met. Not meeting a deadline for a report due to a teacher. Not completing chores around the house prior to a parent coming home from work. Not completing a project within the allotted time frame provided by your superiors at work. All of these examples likely resulted in not making the proper decisions needed to be made to facilitate the tasks necessary. Because decisions were not made and there was likely a lack of proactive planning, "IF" got involved when presenting your reasons to your teacher, parent or boss.

Assume for a moment you are in sales and completed a sales presentation for a potential client. You phone your boss to advise the presentation is completed. You boss inquires as to how you believe it went and whether the purchase agreement will be signed. In response you advise everything went off without a hitch. You then explain there were two things you realized you neglected to mention in the presentation however, they are minor. They may be minor or in the event the agreement is not signed because of the omission, they may become major.

Why did you recall things you may have omitted from the presentation, after it was over? Could this be due to not following a plan? In the event we assume you did have a plan going into the presentation the question would then become whether the plan was written down. Provided the plan was written the next question to ponder is, "Was if followed?"

The circumstances that lead to not completing the tasks at hand may also result in passing the responsibility on to someone else. "Passing the buck" and not accepting responsibility for ones' own actions or omission to act is also common. In the work place blame is often transferred to a newer person on the staff or customer service. The trends in this regard tend to be to attempt to transfer the responsibility to a perceived lower ranked or weaker department. "IF" customer service had done their job effectively the customer would not be upset with the Sales department now.

Now before we go to lunch and think about what has and has not been accomplished on our list for the day, let us reconsider the meaning of "IF." We need to recognize when we are not on track for achieving our goals and adjust accordingly. Provided we are on track we must consider other things we can add to our afternoon agenda to be even more productive. Take into consideration all of your actions and reactions. Do you know with a level of certainty what effect your work has on other people? Every action we take can prompt a reaction from other people. Every exhibited reaction is also an action in and of it self. This can prompt both a reaction and additional action by other people. "IF" we do one thing over another it may generate a completely different result. Remember that "IF" and "DIFERENT" imply plurality.

We talked about "IF" we want to have a good day or a bad day when we first wake up in the morning. We addressed having a "to do" list and highlighting or checking off items as they are completed. Taking into account how what we do affects others needs to always be considered. Making decisions based on analysis and planning is essential. We must not waver from these decisions and base our decision on the facts known to us at the time. Sure this may change later however we cannot second guess ourselves before action is taken on our decisions. The point here is extremely important. The point is that we must take action first and then adjust. Writing down our plans is very important to develop the road map or recipe we need to follow to get us from where we are to where we want to be. Accepting responsibility is essential in developing our own character. Our decisions may prove to be incorrect. People of character can accept this, adapt to the changes needed, revise the written plan and move on. This is not the point where excuses are offered up and then we look the other direction. Fear of making change anchors complacency. Complacency is not an option.

Growth and improvement require change. Change is inherent in everything because as previously stated time is a constant. Time passed will never be regained. Again, complacency is not an option. Growth is the catalyst of change. Knowledge gained transforms our mind and is therefore growth. Change is a constant just as time is a constant.

Chapter Five
Afternoon

Are We Done Yet?

"IF" I did not have turkey for lunch I would not be so tired and ready for a nap. "IF" I did not go to the buffet and over eat I would not have been late returning to the office. "IF" I had not over eaten at the buffet I would be more comfortable to allow me to focus on my job and what I need to accomplish this afternoon. Once again "IF" is being used as a potential excuse or escape route.

Upon returning from lunch there will likely be messages to return, possibly mail to read, emails to respond to and the other tasks on your to do list that have yet to be completed. From the statements above you can see however how we are already potentially creating our way out of regaining the momentum and focus from earlier in the day. Is this because subconsciously we figure by not completing all of the work on our list it will provide for job security? I believe not. We must develop our skills to ride the momentum of our bicycles. One second faster running a lap is progress.

Always strive to do just one more. Push the limits. Push forward and plow your way into the future.

Often times after lunch we are in a slow down mode. We want to work the last few hours of the day and do as little as possible. This may not apply to everyone. Please realize I am making a general statement for example purposes. This may be due to thinking about tasks we need to complete outside the work place and on the way home. Then the magic term pops up again, "IF" I could only leave early to bring the car in for an oil change. "IF" I could get home before everyone else and surprise them by cooking dinner. "IF" enters the mind and sabotages focus and intensity to finish the remaining items on your to do list. This creates fatigue and detracts from your effectiveness.

The early afternoon is an opportunity to make contact with people who were inundated with tasks in the morning and unable to speak to you or even answer the phone. With lunch times varying you may find you have additional quiet time to get work done uninterrupted. This all depends on the nature of the work you do. This circumstance will be different for everyone. Assuming the later of the two and you have time to power through tasks without interruption, take advantage. Get as much done as possible to check off more items on your list or highlight more lines.

Depending on what is remaining on your list for the day, upon your return from lunch, it may be necessary to prioritize your list again. Things may have come up that needed attention in the morning. Review the remaining items and go through the same exercise you completed during your "me time" the night before or that morning. Think about each remaining item and ask yourself if there is a negative consequence to not completing the item today. Those items with consequences are done first. In the event there are a few items that do not have immediate negative consequences, they are not removed from the list but placed lower down on the list. Reprioritize as necessary to maximize your efficiency throughout the day and during your set review periods.

At this point I usually number my remaining items from one to whatever based on the order in which I need to complete the tasks. Keep in mind that this is also where it is very important to do the bigger tasks first because once they are out of the way you will have the time and energy remaining to conquer the smaller items. In the event you do not get to the smaller items and they get forwarded to the next day, they are smaller in nature and will generally be completed faster when you are fresh the next morning. They may be placed lower on the list in the event there are big projects scheduled for that day however, by forwarding them they will not be forgotten. Until there is a negative consequence of inaction toward a task they may be forwarded multiple times. Do not allow yourself to forward a task more than two days consecutively. This would indicate your neglect of completion of the task for three days and by now the task will have negative consequences should it not be completed.

Something important needs to be addressed here. You may have a task that you want to complete right away. The completion is essential but not required until the end of the week. I am using the end of the week for this example but this can be expanded for your monthly, quarterly and yearly goals as well. In such situations I propose you actually determine how many hours will be needed to complete the task. This may be an educated guess based on experience or may require consulting others who have done similar work in the past so as to gauge potential time frames necessary. Once this is done break it up into smaller bite size pieces.

A projection that a task will likely take you three hours to complete can be broken down into three one hour sessions or two one and one half hour sessions over the next few days prior to the due date. By setting a specific appointment for the work you will be focused on completing as much as possible in the time allotted for the appointment. Additionally you will have the piece of mind that you are not neglecting the project or postponing it due to too many other tasks on your to do list. Being it is safe to say these items tend to be the larger projects you will also not get fatigued completing the smaller tasks and possibly not working on the larger projects at all.

As discussed earlier, plan ahead. With effective implementation being practiced these ideas will become habitual. Habits will affect your attitudes and behaviors. Positive attitudes and behaviors exhibited will allow you to be more efficient. You will allow yourself to address unexpected variables that find their way onto your list. Unexpected circumstances will occur. You are in control of your reactions to those circumstances. Welcome the opportunity to excel at what you are good at. Enhance your attitudes and behaviors as well as your opinions and beliefs.

Let's look at a possible hypothetical example. You make a decision to go to lunch at a sandwich shop. You know the store is routinely fast in completing your order and you can swing by the bank to make a deposit around the corner on the way back to the office. The sandwich shop is out of your favorite topping for your meal. The automated teller machine is out of service when you arrive at the bank. You go to the post office to purchase stamps and the line is out the door. Your lunch period is over in ten minutes and the line is too long to wait. The machine in the post office only has packages of one hundred stamps and you only have money to buy ten. You go back to your car and someone has backed up into your car at the post office parking lot. Seeing the wrongdoer you run after them but they are too fast and you cannot get a glimpse of the license plate. No one else will give you the time of day in the parking lot. You ask for witnesses to help you and no one comes to your aid. Inspecting the damages it is discovered it blew out one of your tires. The trunk is opened and filled with duffle bags from softball, items that need to be returned to the hardware store, rentals that need to be returned to the supermarket movie kiosk and dry cleaning. All of this "stuff" is removed to change the tire. The tire is changed and you return to your office and find someone is parked in your assigned parking space. You search for another spot and finally get back to your desk to find an urgent message from your boss. Taking the message to his or her office you are motioned to come in and sit down. The boss is on the phone.

While sitting there you feel a sensation of frustration because of the circumstances that transpired over the past hour. You start to contemplate "IF" thoughts. What did I do to deserve all of this? Who did I make mad? I have so much to do and now I am sitting here being unproductive, why? Maybe I should have gone for Chinese food and not a sandwich. "IF" I had gone to the post office first I would not have been in the wrong place at the wrong time and a victim of hit and run. "IF" is running through your mind to where you are getting a headache as if your brain is the start of the New York Marathon and all the athletes are running across your head.

At this point it would be understandable that one would be less motivated and focused on work or the tasks that need to be done. Contemplating what the boss is going to say then enters your mind. The phone call is obviously not private or you would not have been called into the office to sit down.

Listening to the conversation you sense by the tone of voice your boss is using that they are not happy. Now the "IF" I have something to do with this thought enters your mind. Why is it my fault? This is going to be negative. I am going to get yelled at. This is going to be further demise of the day. You then think you would be better off trying to nail Jello to the wall or eating soup with a fork.

You are likely expecting the worse. The afternoon has not gone according to plan. In review of your planner, schedule, electronic device if you use one, you recognize none of the situations presented in the past two hours was on your schedule. Does this sound familiar? Things happen. Events have taken place, not on your list that needed to be dealt with and thus far you have done so. You contemplate "IF" thoughts relating to what your boss may say and assume they too will be negative. I ask you, Why? To do so is setting your self up with an expectation of a negative. Imposing a self limitation and perspective that because the past couple of hours have been negative the balance of the day will be as well. Circumstances that are beyond our control and beyond our involvement do not require our anticipatory participation in their resolution. A guilty conscious needs no accuser. Once a circumstance is presented to you that require your attention there is no need to invest time with contemplation of the situation and how it relates to you.

This is the further from reality, than you know. In such circumstances it is necessary to confirm the nature of the request to be seen by the boss. It may be negative and another puzzle or opportunity to show your skill sets. It may also be a positive situation. The contemplation of both situations, while still unknown, is not an effective utilization of time or efforts. Do not create anxiety of the unknown. Do not worry about something you have no control over. Instead take control to take a positive action step to deal with the adversities presented to you and show you are more intelligent that the flat tire. If you do not, you are showing that you too have lost your air and pressure necessary to perform your job duties.

We could go into examples of both a positive and negative circumstance with the note left from the boss however, I believe the point is made that there will be variables we all need to deal with on a regular basis that are not planned for. I sincerely hope that not all of the circumstances presented would ever happen to anyone. I especially hope they never happen all at the same time as stated in the example. I do not believe in luck. Luck is success to the lazy. Success is being prepared to take action with the circumstances that are presented to you. The outcome of this action is expected, by you, before starting the action itself, to turn out to be positive and an example of your best work.

To follow the timeline of this discussion it would now be middle to late afternoon. The idea here is to reevaluate the tasks that need to be completed. Regardless of what the boss says, an impromptu "Me Time" needs to be set aside for ten minutes to move forward tasks to the next day and address the items that require immediate attention for that afternoon. As was discussed earlier, it is not likely you would have the luxury of alphabetizing your pens based on color or the names of vendors on them. Today's society is to do everything faster, more efficient, and with fewer materials than ever before. It will not be too much longer before no one remembers only six channels on television or that the televisions were black and white, only. Think about the microwave oven. The first microwave oven in our home was the size of a big screen television today. What about ice makers and water dispensers, cellular telephones and laptop computers. Technologies continue to improve everything to make them smaller, better and in some cases less expensive. The point here is to take time to regroup whenever necessary. A clear mind will allow you to focus more intently and be more productive. As a leader this will set an example for your staff showing them you are effective at this technique.

Whenever variables attack you may need to take out some "Me Time" and regroup. Additional tasks that may need to be added to the list from this example would be to call your insurance company, arrange for a rental car, etc. Approach the situation with an, "Okay stuff happened; let me re-prioritize what needs to be done to resolve the stuff and get back on track with my other to do items." To do otherwise will drain you of energy and is not necessary.

Chapter Six
Will This Day Ever End?

What a Day!!! Whew thank God that is over with. Have you ever had these thoughts as you are walking out to your car at the end of the work day to go home? It is not likely that all of the things mentioned would occur however, we have all been glad when "one of those days" is finally over. But is it? Your work day may have ended and whether this is done just prior to leaving the office or upon arriving home it will be necessary to set aside a few minutes to review your accomplishments for the day.

You went to the bank, post office etc. and it is necessary to have those items on your list for the day's tasks. One other tool that is often helpful to see where you spend your time is to track it. What I mean by this is to have everything written down and as you complete your tasks or at the end of the day when you review your completed items is to write down the approximate time it took to complete each item. Round off the time and put a number down.

As was suggested previously in relationship to a task that is going to require time but is not due until the end of the week, you may break down the time from three hours in one setting to three one hour sessions. Provided we assume for the moment that tasks of this nature are relatively common, by placing a time on each line for each day, worked, you will be able to track how much time was truly spent on the task. Moving forward you will be more accurate in your time assessments for future projects. You may identify recurring activities can be streamlined by doing them at a different time of day. There are a multitude of revelations you will discover by developing a tracking system.

Thinking about this possibility for a moment, we talked about finding time or making it. When I first started to track my time I was shocked to identify something I would have never realized until it hit me in the face. Just like the fish not realizing it lives in water until it is in the boat, I did not realize I was losing approximately one hour per week or one and one half weeks of work time per year because of the time in which I would walk my dog in the morning. Let me explain this a bit further.

At one point I was walking my dog at 7:00 AM each morning and upon completing the walk I would leave for work. The walk would take, on average, thirty minutes each morning. Every day I would go about the same distance. Routinely I would alternate every other day leaving and going to the right or the left out the front yard, but always up to the park and around the block and back. There was a training session that was taking place at my office and I needed to be there earlier for a few days consecutively. As such I walked my dog at 6:00 AM along the same route. I alternated leaving to the right one morning and the left the next morning. In my review of the tracking of my time I discovered that the walk would only take me fifteen to twenty minutes per morning. I believe the discrepancy was dependent on how many leaves my dog wanted to sniff grass up his nose each day. In reality, at 7:00 AM, more of my neighbors were leaving for work and I would stop to greet them and say good morning. The small talk was consuming additional time. I enjoy my neighbors and speaking to them however an additional week plus per year can be quite a bit of production.

The point here is that without tracking the time this routine task was being completed I would be consuming quite a bit of time over the course of a year. With fifty to sixty minutes per week saved it would not sound like a big deal at first. Over the course of fifty-two weeks in a year it equates to fifty-two hours. With an ideal work week being forty hours of work, fifty-two is one and one half weeks over the course of the year, give or take. Let me ask you this, "How much work can you complete in one week without any interruptions of any kind.?"

Depending on your answer to that question, personally, think about an office with only ten employees. With each employee acquiring an additional six working days per year or rounding down to one week, an office is increasing production by five thousand two hundred hours per year, per ten employees. Two thousand eighty hours of work is full time labor in one year. This would be like adding more than two more employees. Now think about tracking time and the question, "Is tracking time important?"

Ten to fifteen minutes per day can add up to quite a bit in the long run. Set aside every evening time to review your accomplishments for the day. This is a good time to forward possible incomplete items to the next day. An opportunity for reflection will allow you to clarify your "IF" thoughts from the day. Think about everything you did during the day and ask your self the question "IF" I did things differently would there have been a different outcome? Analyze what could be done differently to streamline the time invested in the tasks you did. Consider alternatives to improve your results in the event those tasks ever need to be repeated.

The activity review is a time for reflection. Reflect upon the day as you would memories of viewing a movie or going to a professional sports team game. Memories are the learning blocks to allow for adaptation in the future. Take a look at the items on your list for the next day and prioritize. You will feel better once this is done as you will have a foundation for forward progress.

Recognize planning is an on going process. As stated, growth requires change. Are you willing and ready to accept change? Coming to the fork in the road does not warrant panic. Here is an opportunity to review your plan, your road map. Look at the big picture by unfolding the map one more section. Do not create limitations for your self by not opening up the map to see beyond the immediate.

These principles of planning and review are extended outward to the week, the month and the year. Goals involve partly breaking down the individual steps necessary to achieve the long term success desired. What ever you want is achievable with the proper plan. Fulfillment requires focus and dedication. When you bring our magic word into the equation, "IF" Imaginary Falsehood, you are setting yourself up for disappointment and failure. Failure is a gift. Failure is a learning opportunity. Focus and dedication will allow you to pick up where you left off, do the task over more intelligently so as to ensure success and eliminate what you know does not work.

CHAPTER SEVEN
COMMUNICATIONS & THOUGTS

Thus far I have been discussing and providing examples of how certain decisions may affect our point of view and perspectives relating to our day to day activities. The bottom line is we all have choices to make. We are all in control of our choices. Granted we may not always make the best decisions when we look back in hindsight however, recognizing the circumstances that transpired will help identify areas of opportunity to improve. Additionally this recognition will provide a lesson in what not to do and what does not work.

Take a look at the word "Failure." From a communications perspective this may depict certain characteristics depending on the interpretation of the individual. All communications is based on perception. There are many instances where words and terms are subject to the interpretation of the recipient and not the sender of the message. As such, when you are the actual sender of the message what steps are taken to ensure the understanding of the message delivered?

Just as structuring your day and taking time out to evaluate your progress it is equally important to evaluate your communications. Communications is a two way street. To be effective at work we must consider how our actions and reactions may affect others. With communications in the work place, or anywhere for that matter, consider who your audience is. This requires a consideration of the term "IF." We must always validate understanding to be effective.

In too many instances in the corporate world I have witnessed messages being delivered by management to their staff where hours later the manager comes out of their office and what was expected was not being done. The manager will likely go to the person the instructions were given and ask what is happening. It is at this point the manager realized the message they thought they were communicating effectively was not interpreted to have the same meaning.

Clarification of communications is of paramount importance to increase productivity within a workplace. Additionally the act of clarification will save time by reducing the need to start over fresh consuming more time. Time may not be the only component lost. Materials utilized may also be lost. This affects profitability. Circumstances like these may lead to finger pointing and a reduction in morale and camaraderie. Hopefully this would be short lived. This is a two way street for management and their staff. This is a two way street for any communication within the confines of a work environment or at home. Culpability exists with everyone.

When there is a misunderstanding, and we have all had them, it is usually due to one of two potential circumstances. One, there was no clarification of the delivered message being understood properly by the recipient. Two, the recipient understood the instructions given and made a decision to "cut corners" or do it their own way and only adopt a portion of the message. When this occurs there must be accountability. As a manager, a parent, co-worker, partner, it is imperative to have the buy in from the recipients to follow the instructions given. The culpability to ensure success comes from the recipient to discuss their ideas.

When clarification is not sought you may wind up trying to see your fingers on the other side of a glass you are holding that someone else has just filled with milk. You know your thumb is facing you and you know your other fingers are wrapped around the glass but you just cannot see them. Think for a moment to a time when you were in elementary school with a substitute teacher. There may be time you can recall when your regular teacher or the substitute stepped out of the class momentarily. What happened in the class room? Chaos! Everyone started talking and doing what they were not likely supposed to do. The teachers knew the students were in the class room but could not see them. Trying to see your fingers through the glass of milk are similar. You know they are there but cannot see what they are doing.

When there are instructions received and, assuming the position of the recipient, there are thoughts or ideas that differ from those instructions, they should be presented to the person delivering the message in a neutral perspective. As a manager or leader it is essential to get the buy in from the people you are leading when a change is presented or instructions given. In the eventuality there is resentment or the actions requested are not fully understood there will be less motivation to do the task at all. This may also lead to lower morale and less focus. This may jeopardize quality control. These issues may hurt the organization in both the short term and long run.

With this seed of thought planted I would like to briefly discuss expectations. We all have expectations when we go to a restaurant. For clarification purposes let us assume you are going to a pizza restaurant. What is your expectation when your pizza is delivered to your table? Here comes the "IF." "IF" the pizza was burnt would you accept it? "IF" the pizza was prepared but never placed into the oven to be cooked and was brought to your table raw, would you accept it? Both of these situations would not meet your expectation of having a hot pizza brought to your table for your meal.

Certain expectations should not require clarification. Let us now take this extreme one step further. You decide to patronize this same pizza restaurant again a few weeks later. This time you place your order and indicate you want a fully cooked, non burnt pizza brought to your table. Would this seem ridiculous? We all probably know better than to have this expectation but the point is that we would consider the past failure we experienced in conjunction with the contemplation of our favorite word, "IF" and handled the situation differently. Knowing what did not work in the past we would prepare and set our expectations up in a new way.

Having spent many years in the insurance claims industry there were always goals and objectives set for the individual departments and office as a whole. At one point early in my career there was a customer service issue surrounding supplements being processed. Let me explain a few things for clarification purposes for those who may not have an understanding of insurance claims. I worked in the physical damage department, at the time. This department or unit was responsible for going out to the location where the damaged cars were located after an accident. This may be an auto body repair facility, a tow yard, and sometimes a customers' home or office. The responsibility was to write an estimate for the cost of repairs to the vehicle and take photos to document the damages resulting from the accident. Now this is also very important because there is often unrelated damage to a car that is in the proximity of damages from the accident. This is an entirely separate issue however, and can lead to customer service issues. A customer may have an expectation that everything wrong on their car is repaired when only the damages from the loss are part of the claim.

Anyway, relating to the damages, as externally damaged parts are removed from the vehicle for repair or replacement it is often realized there was additional damage that could not be seen. The repair shops would call the appraiser back out to the shop to write a supplement. This may result in a delay in continuing repair to the vehicle. This was often less likely to be a major issue. The other type of supplement that usually created an issue was when there were cost increases for parts purchased. Parts manufacturers would raise the costs on the parts quite often. While the parts prices were often updated each month it posed potential issues late in the month. When I first started in the industry there were books and they were updated quarterly and not monthly. Anyway, the management team tracked our turn around time on processing supplements. It was stated quite clearly the supplements needed to be processed within two days. A new expectation was being established between management and the staff. This was aggressive to those in the field. This expectation that was aggressive to the field staff was completely unreasonable to the customers.

When supplements were received for part price increases every invoice for every part purchased on the estimate were needed for review. In the more recent times where everything was computerized the corrections were entered into the computerized estimate to generate the supplement. Some of the files this was quick and simple. Larger repairs took much longer. The main server was communicated with, electronically, several times per day. The idea was this; after each estimate the server was contacted so the file would be available to the staff inside the claims office. This in turn would remove the estimate from the representative's laptop. In order to have the estimate visible by the office staff the estimate first went through a cycle of being on the main server. The estimate was then attached to the appropriate claims file based on a suffix on the claim number that indicated which office the individual claim was being handled through. Turn around time could vary from less than an hour to one day.

When a supplement was received it was usually faxed to the office. The management wanted them processed immediately believing they would therefore improve customer service. This is true however it was requiring representatives to delay seeing the cars on the new claims in a timely manner. This upset the customers that just had an accident. It was a vicious circle. Supplement processing improved but expeditious inspections of new claims suffered. There was no balance. We were straddling the fence and kept falling. I am sure you can imagine straddling a fence and falling and how that may affect your morale or attitude.

Another issue related to the part price increase supplements not being processed quickly was the fact the shop would not release the car to the customer until they were paid for the repairs they completed. To do otherwise was a liability to the shop because they no longer had collateral for the work they did. You cannot pick up your dry cleaning without paying for it. The customer service for the office was suffering because supplements were not being processed quickly. Customer service suffered because freshly damaged cars were not being inspected either.

As was stated some of the supplements were faster than others to process. The main server was communicated with on a regular basis with the minimum being once per day. So as to not consume time and be less efficient every time a supplement came in, and I was communicating with the main server, I recalled the original estimate in order to have it back on my laptop. I may not have been able to process the supplement that moment but there were plenty of opportunities during the day where I was early for an appointment or waiting for a bumper to be removed from a vehicle to try and avoid supplements to begin with and see what could be hidden damage. This afforded the opportunity to process supplements. See, I refused to sit idle and wait. In the event I was waiting for a part to be removed, a shop to find keys to a car, pry open a hood or whatever I would work on other things concurrently. I would work on my supplements.

Once I started to recall any known supplements and they were staring me in the face every time I looked at my computer I was able to process them within one day. I was still able to see all of the new cars assigned to me. My results improved. Customer satisfaction improved. At first all of the representatives were shaking our heads that it was impossible to meet the criteria. The response we received was to find a way to do it. There was no buy in from the staff. There was no support offered. Management issued a directive and no more.

The communication was one sided. There was no discussion. When it was realized that this was a more efficient way to stay on top of the supplements that were pending I shared it with management. They questioned it at first and I proposed I show it to a representative from another office and have them pilot test the theory. This was done with two representatives from two adjacent offices. All of a sudden within a few weeks their results were also improving. At this point it was implemented company wide and it became a protocol. Now I am sure there were representatives that chose to do the supplements on their own time at home at night or on the weekends. I refused to work at night or on the weekends. This was my time. I earned the time. I wanted there to be balance between my personal and professional life. A way and method was found.

The expectations presented were not clearly communicated. I learned from this experience for when I became a manager and needed to deliver similar types of messages to my staff. Recognizing what was effective and what presented resentment in communications of expectations was very important. This helped me redirect my staff with more efficiency.

Necessity is the mother of all inventions. This, for me, was another wow, "I could have had a V8" moment. I simply realized I was communicating with the server multiple times throughout the day. I also realized I had down time waiting for a hood to be opened, or a wheel to be removed from a car to view the suspension. It made sense. It was an issue of working smarter and not harder. This was a decision I made. It was a choice.

I could have contemplated, "IF" and made the decision to hinder my effectiveness in seeing cars on the new claims. Had I done this it would have resulted in not meeting the expectations established for this portion of my job. Another choice I could have made would have been the decision to sacrifice my personal time with my family to accomplish the objectives surrounding the supplements. Yet another choice was to do nothing and go about my business. This would not help remedy anything and likely create other management instituted protocols to be handed down in an effort to repair customer service results. The likelihood of anything being remedied was not very good with any of the scenarios presented.

With the mind set that the customers were paying my salary I figured I must do my best to create a win / win situation for everyone. The bottom line with this example is that I made choices. I made decisions that were later adopted as protocol. All of the representatives had their own style and it was clearly not meeting the objectives desired for customer service.

In observing the styles of my co-workers from my office and my sister offices I was able to learn what was effective and less effective. I observed what was taking place and our individual styles. With this I created a simple spread sheet to track categories that I could measure. This was based on what I perceived to have an effect on our customer service results. Armed with this knowledge I went to war. The war, was the fight to find a solution to improving our results. The battle was determining which way to go when I came to the fork in the road. Fortunately based on my observations and analysis I made the correct decision. Once you have the required information to make a decision, just make it. Should your decision be wrong, work backwards to the point where you know everything worked properly based on the tracking. Learn by it. Once successful, hone it, polish it, nurture it and share it.

At this point I would expect a circumstance could be recalled where a directive was issued by management to improve, fix, repair, change or whatever a process within your organization or department. When you think about it, there was likely a statement made without additional instructions provided to how to actually accomplish what was requested. Expectations are often expressed in generalities and not based on comprehensive thought and clear communications. Without both, you may as well bail water from a sinking boat with a tea spoon. You will not be efficient or successful. Expectations are often communicated by management to subordinates based on insufficient consideration of "IF" and consequences associated with the communication. Also short of being considered in the equation is the validation of understanding of the communication presented. Simply being aware of this point next time you have to communicate a message or expectation to someone else you will be more effective.

When directives are given it is essential the communication is clear. The communication must then be validated by the person delivering the message that it is understood in the manner in which it was intended. To do otherwise is a futile attempt to pacify upper management. When expectations are set they must be explained, like anything else, and the tools necessary must be provided to achieve the results desired. Without providing the tools, instructions on the use of the tools, and a monitoring system for the implementation, there will likely be less success and more shortcomings and frustrations experienced. This may all be avoided with proper planning and communications.

Several times validation or verification of the communicated message has been mentioned. In my observations and experiences the best way to facilitate this is to ask questions. Ask the recipient of your message to paraphrase what you have said so you can validate understanding and avoid mishaps. When this is done from a neutral and non accusatory perspective you will substantially improve your results. Equally you will save time, money and materials. Be careful not to be condescending or imply the recipient of your communication is stupid or something. Set up the conversation with your confidence in the persons' ability and skill sets to achieve the objective desired. Continue at the beginning with an explanation that the project is very important and once all of the instructions are given that you expect both feed back on ideas of how the implementation may be done better and or repeating the instructions to avoid issues later due to the importance of the assignment. This will make the recipient feel more involved and essential to the outcome. Additionally with the importance placed on the serious nature of the assignment, staff members will often feel a sense of pride in the confidence you are placing in them and therefore be more attentive to the instructions you are providing.

Chapter Eight
Planning Ahead

Planning is the key to success. With communication in the work place, just as at home, it is essential to take a step back and think about the purpose of the message. What is it that you want to say? How will it be stated? What will the reception of the message likely be? What is the intended perception of the message you desire? Will the person be defensive, thankful, offended, upset, thrilled, or excited with the message? These are all considerations that must be contemplated. The contemplation of these items may affect "IF" you deliver the message in the morning or evening. "IF" may be a consideration of having a witness with you in the event this is a disciplinary issue to be delivered to a staff member. Especially in the event the staff member is the opposite gender, you may wish to have another manager or supervisor with you, if not human resources.

When we go on vacation it is first determined where we want to go. This can be affected by many different elements or examples of "IF." A trip around the world may be nice to some people, "IF" they have the time that can be missed from work. We do not need to mention costs as I believe the point is clear. "IF" has a great deal to do with where you plan to go on vacation. Once it is decided where you want to go you can then plan. The planning involves a decision on which mode of transportation you may take. What are the cost differences in driving versus flying three hundred miles? It may be faster to fly but cost more money for the tickets and then you still need ground transportation upon your arrival. This may affect other funding issues for your trip.

The horse is already dead so we do not need to beat it any further. I believe the point is made that there is a great deal surrounding the term "IF." When we go to the super market without a list I propose we spend more time in the market itself. I believe that without a market list we will also spend more money because we may purchase items impulsively. This may lead us to forget what we truly needed to purchase to begin with and precipitate yet another trip to the market because we do not have all of the ingredients we needed to bake our cake or make our bread. "IF" we plan ahead and think about potential consequences before reacting to a situation we will be more efficient. "IF" our decision was to sit down and make a list and then go to the market we would have been more effective.

This is not to say that there may be opportunities where we must react to a situation and do not have the time to contemplate consequences. In such a situation we may make the wrong decision or react inappropriately. This will serve as a learning experience. We must keep a positive open mind to wrong decisions that we make and recognize them as a learning opportunity.

One of the most important elements to effective planning is to write it down. Written plans offer a blue print of your steps you will take. By doing this you provide a measuring system to track your progress toward your goal. This will act as a reference later. It is even more important to have this when the decisions made are wrong. A written plan allows you to go back and review where the errors were made and you then know up to what point you were successful. This is similar to what I had done with the supplements issue at the insurance company.

Let us assume momentarily there is a project that needs to be completed in your office. There are multiple departments involved with the project and this affects the entire company not merely your office. A directive comes down to you from corporate and you implement it without a plan. The departments are given instructions and each department is responsible for a portion of the project. There is a due date when this project needs to be back to the corporate office. The deadline is missed. Why?

You look back at the directive and know you told everyone what was required. One department that only had a small percentage of the total project was inundated with new customer orders or issues and failed to complete their section of the project. The supervisor or manager of the unit is called into your office, as the manager, to determine why. It is discovered that the supervisor recalls the directive being delivered two months prior but was so busy with the new orders and issues that it was accidentally forgotten. Is this reasonably accurate? Does this happen from time to time? Could this happen? I believe absolutely on all counts.

Let me assure you this happens more often than not. We all get busy. There was no plan on the part of the manager to follow up with the department supervisor to calibrate the status of the project well enough in advance to correct the fact it was completely forgotten about. The result in this circumstance is a missed deadline. The solution is simple.

A clearly defined expectation needed to be communicated to the supervisor of the department. A plan needed to be established that allowed for a check point to confirm the status of the progress. A note written on a calendar to follow up would provide for a simple plan.

There is culpability on the part of both the manager and the supervisor in this example. Having been in both roles I believe there was more responsibility on the part of the manager than the supervisor. Both were negligent in their respective duties. A written plan does not have to be elaborate.

A written plan should identify what needs to be achieved, when it will be completed, who is involved, why you want to achieve the goal and where it will take the organization. The five "W's" of a goal will help you set up the road map or write the recipe for success. There are other more involved and detailed techniques I work on with my clients however, this is a strong foundation to ensure you will stay on track and not miss a deadline in the future.

Chapter Nine
Home Stretch!

In summary, "IF" is a very small word however it carries a tremendous weight and influence on daily activities. Realize that "IF" you do nothing, nothing happens. Time will pass. Time is the only thing that we have that costs us nothing to obtain yet we never invest it. The perception we often carry relating to time is that we can make time to do something. Another perception surrounding time is that we can buy time. Create the circumstances you desire.

We may all make mistakes because we selected the wrong "IF." We contemplate in hindsight that we should have taken the other fork in the road or made a different decision. Reflect back on the story about the two brothers for a moment. Being a fictional scenario let us assume for a moment the outcome of the two brothers meeting up again on the plane allowed for them to return home and begin the rebuilding process of the family relationships that had been destroyed. What is the potential outcome of such a scenario? It would depend on many contemplations and thoughts surrounding 'IF."

Negativity cannot enter our minds unless we open the door. Disappointments and failures are expected in life but they do not have to be final nor fatal. When we have the will and desire to complete something and write a plan to achieve the desired goal there is nothing that can stop us. There are too many "IFs" in life to sit back and wait. Power is nothing when it is not utilized effectively. Atrophy will set in when we do not use our muscles. Why do we allow ourselves to diminish our effectiveness because of a two letter word, "IF?"

Here is a thought for you, "IF" you do not apply new remedies to existing circumstances you will develop immunity to progress. This being said my question to you becomes, "What are you waiting for?" The question of life is "IF." There are too many things in the world we can ponder and never find an answer that will be universally acceptable. My thoughts expressed in this book are likely to cause disagreement among many. These are my thoughts and my intent, as stated before, is merely to inspire thoughts in others and share mine. It is up to each and every one of us to want to give our best all of the time. Short term disappointments should not deter us from our goals but inspire us to discover a new "IF." Try something new and never settle.

The most successful people fail the most too. Babe Ruth may have hit the most home runs but also struck out the most. "IF" he were afraid of strike outs every time he went to the plate, what would the outcome have been for him? Look upon failures as a gift. You have isolated what does not work. Never settle or compromise. No one can ever tell you your dreams are wrong. Your feelings are yours. You are entitled to your feelings and beliefs. No one can ever tell you your goals are too big. Goals may be aggressive and simply require a different plan for different people. That plan may include a different time frame. Time is something we do not control. We can only control ourselves within time. With this point made, there is no time like the present to start working on your goals. Start by deciding what goals you want to focus on. Next will be the task of writing them down. With them written down there is a tangibility attached to them. We never know when our time may be up. You have now provided a legacy to have others continue with your goal and plan should anything happen to you.

Perspective influences everything we do. To look at something is one thing but to truly see that same thing implies a different level of understanding. When that understanding is then extracted and shared to offer insight to someone else, this is when there is validation that we have truly recognized the learning opportunity in what we have seen. The act of sharing information is what expands us as individuals. Sharing what we have discovered individually is what helps society become better. We can choose to be one of those types of people that make things happen, watch things happen or wonder what has happened. This is all dependent on our interpretations of the word "IF." Remember what was stated at the beginning of the book, the word "IF" implies choice. Choice implies plurality. Plurality implies there may be differences in our choices. Recognize the word "different" contains the word "IF."

Let me share with you some quick random thoughts relating to perspectives. When people are rude to you at work it is not likely because of what you did but what the people before you did. Therefore when you are dealing with your customers and want to make a difference you must recognize that small things do count and two thirds of promotion is motion. Go above and beyond your defined objectives and expectations for your job title every chance you get. When opportunities to go above and beyond are not present, make them. Make decisions and follow through. Had Christopher Columbus turned around no one would have remembered him. What you see and attend to your mind will consider. Attend to everything possible. What becomes consideration will often times develop beliefs and once you believe in your considerations you will be prepared to take action. Do not dwell once you have the information needed to make a decision. Make the decision and take action and you are done. It will always be better to try something and fail than to never try anything at all and succeed.

Think about the most successful business you possibly can. Now think about how this business started. Any business you may have thought of started the same way. It started with a thought. The founder of that business likely had contemplations around the term "IF." Look where it got them. Depending on the business there were likely struggles and set backs. These did not stop the entrepreneurial train from leaving the station. "IF" it had you would not have thought of the business.

The best way to get something done is to simply begin. You can come up with all the rules you want relating to success and achievement but they all require a start. When you are at work do not simply grin and bear a situation that is presented to you. Smile, take pride, take action and do your best work. Make your work ethic a standard to prepare for living in the future and not reliving the past. To be more successful at your job have the courage to stand up as a leader and take action where others are afraid to even stand up. Your obstacles you perceive are more threatening when you take your eyes off your objective or goal.

Opportunities abound. They are not circumstances where you will get something for nothing however. Too many times opportunities are missed by those missing opportunities.

Be prepared to look in all directions and not merely go through life looking through the rear view mirror at what is possibly chasing you. Success comes in cans and failures come in cants. The doors to opportunity are wide open when you are looking in the direction of the right doors. What is required is that you persevere to establish your commitment to yourself and recognize your known abilities. View the possible as probable and this simple perception correction will take you from where you are to where you have never been. Think before you act. Think before you speak. Do not speak unless your words positively enhance the silence otherwise enjoyed by no words being said. Neither success nor failure is permanent. The ball is in your court and it is always your next move. Learn not to complain when the ball is dropped and you were the last one to have it. Anything you wish to accomplish can be with the proper mind set. Be who and what you are. This is what people need to recognize and accept. Someone else's reality does not need to influence your reality unless you choose to let it. Recognizing what you are is the first step to being able to know what you do not wish to be and being able to avoid it. Learn from your past in order to inherit the future. Adversity is an awesome teacher. In business never forget that business itself is a game, money is the score, and the game is never over.

To wrap things up I want to share with you something I wrote for my son. In 2005 I wrote this for my son who was ten at the time. Below is a copy of the poem or writing. Remember what I said earlier about having a plan and putting the plan into writing to create a legacy. This writing speaks to both of these issues in my own way.

Aaron E. Danchik, President

Motivate Others To Make It Matter

A dream is an individual thing.

With or without dreams we may wander aimlessly,

With dreams put into action, we are more likely to aim at the dream itself.

Create your own legacy now, for in the end it will not matter what you did.

It will not matter what you gained or what you had.

It will not matter if you owed, or if you were owed.

What will matter is what you leave behind.

What will matter is not what tangibles are left but the intangibles left behind.

What will matter is how your character and integrity are spoken of.

Why wait to find out what will matter?

Make a difference today. Teach people what you know,

Learn from others with an open mind and accept others for who and what they are and stand for.

Be a person of character, integrity and ethics,

A person such as this is motivating. A person such as this matters.

Motivate others to emulate your actions not just your words.

Be true to your word and create your own legacy.

Act now for how you want to be remembered as this motivates and is what matters.

Dream the impossible, create the I'm Possible.

You are in control and the Captain of your own ship.

Inaction will anchor complacency and complacency is not an option!

Live to your word and you will be successful.

This will motivate and this will matter.

Who in your life is your motivation?

Live for them and build your legacy.

This will motivate and this will matter.

As I have indicated several times in this book, the message written is my opinion. I am grateful for the feedback I have received from my clients, to date. I am grateful for what I have and not jealous of what other people have. Provided my little book has inspired one person to look at things differently and see things in a new light I have achieved my objective.

I came to the realization coaching young kids in track and field that I wanted to help anyone I possibly could develop a plan to achieve their individual goals. I could write or tell numerous stories about kids I have coached. I could equally write or tell numerous stories about businesses I have worked with. Let me leave you with one more closing thought.

It is never too late to begin laying the foundation to build what you have always wished you could be. When you dare yourself to take action you will win more often than those who do not dare at all. None of us truly knows how long we have on earth. When you are scared use it to your advantage to look fear in the face and confront it. Often times the fear is equally afraid of you. Animals attack humans because they are afraid of us. Usually this is when we infringe upon their territory. They use their fear as a motivation to protect their territory. This motivation leads to an attack. The animal often wins. Now think about this, are you smarter than a wild animal? Do you have more education than a wild animal? What is your perspective relating to fear? Use it as a motivation to take action. The sense of accomplishment when we conquer a fear is tremendous.

Challenges can cause us to run and hide or further develop our character. It is our perspective we bring to the situation. "IF" applies to everything we do. "IF" we want a d-IF-ferent outcome based on our perspective we need to take the action to bring it about. Consider for a moment a simple mathematical question. "IF" you had four items, what percentage would two of those items equal? "IF" you had four quarters, how much would two quarters add up to? I truly hope you were able to come up with fifty percent.

Remember LIFE is 50% IF!

IF shows there is more than one!

We have choices. Choices are based on differences! IF resides in differences!

What is your perspective?

What will your perspective be?

How will you communicate your ideas in the future?

It is a proven statistic that many executives work IN their business not ON their business. This is due to more complex issues businesses currently face day in and day out. I spent over seventeen years witnessing the outcome of decisions made believing change would produce a desired result. Then the realization that *time was poorly invested* because other changes still needed to be made resulted in diminishing morale by implementing more changes shortly after the first change.

Based on spaced repetition learning, focus on positive behavioral changes within employees, and applied accountability, my programs allow clients to do their jobs better utilizing more of their true potential. This increases morale, camaraderie, communications and overall effectiveness within organizations.

Realizing your organization has extensive training and is successful, the question becomes, how will this be maintained? A high level of consistency and success is paramount to any business entity. It costs considerably more to acquire a new client than retain existing clients. Please allow your training department to focus on the fundamental functions of your industry. Allow an *outside source* to develop the skills that will allow for the fundamental functions to be implemented by your staff while not investing in another full time staff member in your training department. *By using an outside source you will not incur fees associated with vacations, holidays or a benefits package*.

To identify *only a few* of the programs available, one program surveys organizations to validate the employees' satisfaction with the company and areas of potential concern based on your employees' perspective. Additionally, programs are available in:

Time Management	Sales	Leadership
Communication	Team Building	Decision Making
Supervision	Management	Customer Service
Call Center Training	Expectations	Hiring/employee Retention
Prioritization	Ethics/integrity	Presentation Preparation

I invite you to contact me at *818-730-8505* to set up a mutual evaluation discussion of no more than one half hour to show how there is a GUARANTEED Return on Investment with these programs. No benefits packages are paid and no vacation. The programs are developed, implemented and monitored with minimal disruption to your work flow and staff.

Synchronized

Solutions

Synchronizing YOUR Actions to be
Solutions to Achieve YOUR Dreams!
Business Coaching

Aaron E. Danchik
President

5302 Jon Dodson Drive
Agoura Hills, CA 91301
818-730-8505   818-991-1892 Fax
www.synchronizedsolution.com
info@synchronizedsolution.com

About the Author

Aaron Danchik is the President and founder of Synchronized Solutions--www.synchronizedsolution.com—Following his graduation from Pepperdine University and having worked multiple jobs throughout school he found himself working in the Insurance claims industry for over fourteen years.

A desire had always rested deep within Aaron to coach and mentor people he worked with as well as in sports. Living in Agoura Hills, California with his wife Sherry and son Blake and their dog, he began to coach youth track and field. Giving the credit to his son for bringing his true desires to the conscious level of his thought he began a business consulting and coaching business. Taking his experience as an employee of a large corporation and having worked his way up from an entry level to a management position, Aaron focused on development of his staff and team building.

Taking this knowledge and experience and wanting to share the difficulties identified over the years, the desire is to help others avoid the same difficulties while setting an example for his son. The example is that any goal you desire to achieve can be achieved with the proper vehicle and plan.

Printed in the United States
75265LV00001BA/133-258